Contents – Qu

Contents – Answers

Test Cricket Part One

1) England lost their first Test Match of the 21st century by an innings and 37 runs away from home against which team in January 2000?

2) Which bowler took four wickets in one over versus the West Indies in August 2000?

3) Pakistan forfeited the fourth Test in August 2006 after being accused of ball tampering at which English ground?

4) Which player took 7/12 in the First Test against the West Indies in Kingston in 2004 as England claimed a ten wicket victory?

5) Alec Stewart scored a hundred in his 100th Test against which country at Old Trafford in the year 2000?

6) During the 2009/10 tour of South Africa, which number 11 batsman twice had to survive in the final over of the game to save matches for England?

7) In which year did Brian Lara score his world record 400 runs against England?

8) Which South African scored consecutive double hundreds in the 1st and 2nd Tests of their 2003 tour of England?

9) Wicket-keeper Geraint Jones was born in which country?

10) Muttiah Muralitharan became the leading wicket-taker of all time in Test cricket when he passed Shane Warne by claiming which England batter as his 709th victim in December 2007?

11) Which legendary West Indian fast bowler played his final Test against England at the Oval in August 2000?

12) Which Pakistani batsman was comically out hit-wicket by falling onto his stumps after attempting a sweep off Monty Panesar at Headingley in 2006?

13) Led by captain Andrew Flintoff, England won the 3rd Test away in India in 2006 to claim a memorable 1-1 draw in the series, but which veteran off-spinner took the final wicket of the series?

14) England collapsed to an innings and 23 run defeat when they were bowled out for 51 in their second innings against which team in February 2009?

15) Which England bowler ended the victory over South Africa in the 4th Test at Johannesburg in 2005 with a match-winning contribution of 12 wickets?

16) Who took charge of his first Test Match as England coach against the West Indies in 2007?

17) Which England bowler took a wicket with the first ball of the Test when he dismissed Daren Ganga of the West Indies at Chester-le-Street in June 2007?

18) Which legendary South African batsman did James Anderson dismiss to claim his 100th Test wicket in 2008?

19) England claimed a memorable series victory away against Pakistan in 2000, with which two batsmen finishing not out as they chased down the total in near darkness in the 3rd and final Test?

20) Michael Vaughan lost his wicket by what unusual mode of dismissal during the 1st innings of the 3rd Test against India in Bangalore in 2001?

One Day Internationals Part One

1) Who hit five sixes off the final five balls of the innings off the bowling of Yuvraj Singh in an ODI against India in 2007?

2) Against which country did England sneak home by one wicket thanks to a small partnership between Darren Gough and Alan Mullally in February 2000?

3) England tied the final of the NatWest Series at Lord's against which team in 2005?

4) Which off spinner took a stunning catch to dismiss Shane Watson in the second final of the 2007 Commonwealth Bank series in Australia?

5) Which bowler agonisingly missed out on a hat-trick on his ODI debut against Bangladesh in 2005 when his hat-trick delivery bounced on top of the stumps but did not remove either bail?

6) New Zealand claimed a last ball victory in a controversial match in 2008 which was played in a tense atmosphere after which New Zealand batsman was controversially run out after colliding with Ryan Sidebottom?

7) England tied with South Africa at Bloemfontein in February 2005 after which bowler restricted the hosts to seven off the final over, despite seeing a no-ball hit for four off his first delivery?

8) Which seamer took a remarkable 5 for 15 off ten overs against Zimbabwe in January 2000?

9) England lost a day/night match away from home against which country by one run in January 2000?

10) Nasser Hussain scored his highest one-day score of 115 in a thrilling match against which country in the 2002 NatWest Series final?

11) England conceded a match versus which team at Headingley in June 2001 after a pitch invasion towards the end of the game?

12) James Kirtley took a sensational diving catch with his left hand in a 2002 ODI versus which side?

13) England lost a one-day international against the West Indies at Lord's in July 2004 despite which two players scoring hundreds for them that day?

14) Which all-rounder claimed figures of 6 for 31 off his ten overs in a match versus against Bangladesh in 2005?

15) Against which country did Kevin Pietersen make his England ODI debut in 2004?

Twenty 20's

1) Which England bowler took four wickets in the T20 victory in England's first ever match in the format, beating Australia before the Ashes series in 2005?

2) Who scored 103 off 51 balls against New Zealand in November 2019?

3) Which bowler successfully defended 17 runs in the super over after England and New Zealand had tied another match, this time a T20 in 2019?

4) England beat the West Indies by 1 run in the 2nd match of their 2022 tour despite which bowler conceding 28 runs off the last over of the match?

5) England were skittled out for just 80 when chasing 171 for victory against which team in 2012?

6) England fought back to beat Australia by two runs in the 1st T20 in September 2020, thanks in part to who bowling the last over of the match and securing the win?

7) Chris Woakes conceded only 7 runs in the final over as England beat which side by 3 runs away from home in November 2015?

8) Which bowler claimed four wickets and only conceded six runs against the West Indies in 2019?

9) In the next match of that series another England player took four wickets, this time for seven runs, but who was it?

10) Despite only chasing 114, England lost by 25 runs to which country in September 2011?

11) Which veteran Sri Lankan opener claimed the man of the match award as England lost for the first time in T20 internationals in June 2006?

12) Which country did England beat 3-0 in an away series in late 2020?

13) Which Australian opener smashed 156 off 63 balls in a T20 in 2013 as his team racked up a massive 248/6?

14) South Africa snuck home by running two off the last ball in the 1st match of the 2016 series after which England bowler failed to collect a throw from the deep to effect a run-out?

15) Before becoming head coach of England's white ball team in 2022, Matthew Mott was the coach of which women's national side?

The Ashes Part One

1) At which ground did Mark Butcher score an unbeaten 173 to guide England to victory in the 4th Test in 2001?

2) Who was the top wicket-taker during the 2001 Ashes?

3) Which Australian made 152 in the 1st Test in 2001?

4) Which future Sky Sports Cricket presenter was dropped after the 3rd Test of the 2001 series and never played for England again?

5) Which England bowler was injured in the outfield during the 1st Test of the 2002/03 series?

6) Which Englishman was top scorer in the 2002/03 series in Australia with 633 runs?

7) Who stood in for Alex Stewart as the England wicketkeeper for the 4th Test of the 2002/03 Ashes?

8) Which bowler took seven second innings wickets to lead England to victory in the final Test in 2003?

9) Which four England players scored hundreds during the 2005 Ashes?

10) Which substitute fielder famously ran-out Ricky Ponting during the 4th Test in 2005?

11) How many wickets did Shane Warne take in the 2005 series?

12) At which ground did England win to take a 2-1 lead in the 2005 series?

13) Who scored a double hundred for England at Adelaide in the 2nd Test in 2006?

14) Which two Australians combined to put on a partnership of 279 for the 6th wicket in the 2006 Boxing Day Test?

15) Which Australian pace bowler took 26 wickets in the 2006/07 series, more than anybody else?

16) England clung on for a draw in the 1st Test in 2009 after seeing which four Australians rack up tons in their only innings of the match?

17) Which batter helped keep Australia at bay in that 2009 Test by facing 245 balls in the second innings?

18) With the first two deliveries of day two of the 3rd Test in 2009, which England bowler dismissed Shane Watson and Michael Hussey?

19) England re-claimed the Ashes in 2009, with which player taking the final catch as Graeme Swann dismissed Michael Hussey?

20) What was the final series score in 2009 Ashes?

21) Which three players did Peter Siddle dismiss for his hat-trick during the 1st Test of the 2010/11 series?

22) Simon Katich was run-out in the first over of the 2nd Test in 2010 without facing a ball by which England fielder?

23) At what score did England declare their second innings in the 1st Test of the 2010/11 Ashes?

24) How many runs did Alastair Cook score in the 2010/11 series?

25) Which England bowler took the final wicket of the series in 2010/11, dismissing Michael Beer to claim a 3-1 win?

Captains

1) Who was the permanent England Test Match captain at the start of the 21st century?

2) Graham Thorpe captained England in three One Day Internationals in 2001 against which team?

3) Who stood in as Test captain to replace Michael Vaughan on two occasions, once against New Zealand in 2004 and again versus Pakistan in 2005?

4) In which year did Andrew Strauss first captain the Test side?

5) Kevin Pietersen recorded how many wins as captain of the England Test team?

6) Which off spinner captained England in one T20 match against New Zealand in 2013, although the game was called off after two deliveries?

7) Who was the permanent captain of the T20 side from 2011-2014?

8) Against which team did Joe Root begin his spell as England Test captain?

9) Ben Stokes led England in a Test Match against which country in place of Joe Root in the summer of 2020?

10) Ben Stokes returned to lead the ODI team in a three match series against Pakistan in 2021 after the initial squad was hit by a Covid-19 outbreak, but what was the final score of that series?

First Wickets

Can you name the player these bowlers claimed as their first international wicket from the options given? Remember, this includes Test Matches, ODI's and T20's.

1) Matthew Hoggard
   Brian Lara
   Rahul Dravid
   Younis Khan

2) Simon Jones
   Ajay Ratra
   Anil Kumble
   Zaheer Khan

3) James Anderson
   Mark Vermuelen
   Adam Gilchrist
   Sanath Jayasuriya

4) Graeme Swann
   Kumar Sangakkara
   Gautam Gambhir
   Rahul Dravid

5) Alistair Cook
   Mohammed Shami
   Ishant Sharma
   Bhuvneshwar Kumar

6) Ben Stokes
   Shaun Marsh
   Brad Haddin
   Mitchell Johnson

7) Mark Wood
   Brendon McCullum
   Asad Shafiq
   William Porterfield

8) Craig Overton
   Tim Paine
   Pat Cummins
   Steve Smith

9) Jofra Archer
   Mark Adair
   Paul Stirling
   Andy Balbirnie

10) Matthew Fisher
    Kraigg Brathwaite
    John Campbell
    Jason Holder

50 Over World Cups

1) Andrew Flintoff was suspended by England during which years' World Cup after a drunken incident with a pedalo?

2) Shoaib Akhtar bowled a delivery recorded at over 100mph to which England player during the group stage of the 2003 World Cup?

3) Which Essex player took three wickets in the win over Namibia in 2003?

4) Which Australian took seven wickets in the final Group Stage match as England were eliminated from the 2003 competition?

5) Which three teams did England face in the Group Stage of the 2007 World Cup?

6) Which former and future Ireland international opened the batting for England at the 2007 World Cup?

7) Which England player scored tons versus Australia and West Indies in 2007?

8) In the 2011 competition England tied a Group Stage match against which team?

9) Which Irish player scored a dramatic hundred as England fell to an historic defeat in 2011?

10) Which two Sri Lankans scored unbeaten tons as England were beaten by 10 wickets at the Quarter Final stage in 2011?

11) England won only two of their six matches at the 2015 World Cup as they crashed out at the Group Stage, which teams did they beat?

12) Which batsman was left stranded on 98 not out during England's opening loss to Australia in 2015?

13) Which New Zealand batter scored 77 off 25 balls as they destroyed England in their 2015 meeting?

14) Who was the last man to be dismissed as Bangladesh knocked England out of the 2015 competition by beating them by 15 runs?

15) Ben Stokes took an incredible catch to dismiss which South African in the opening day win in the 2019 World Cup?

16) England lost to Pakistan in the 2019 Group Stage despite which two of their batters scoring hundreds?

17) After England were hit by numerous injuries, who ended up batting at three in the win over the West Indies in 2019?

18) Which side did England beat in their final Group Stage game in 2019 to seal their Semi-Final place?

19) What score did both teams make in their 50 overs as England tied with New Zealand in the 2019 final?

20) Which England player fielded the ball in the deep then threw the ball to Jos Buttler off the last ball of the super over to claim victory for England in the 2019 World Cup Final?

T20 World Cups

1) The first ever T20 World Cup was held in 2007, but which country was the host?

2) In the match with India, Yuvraj Singh hit six sixes off one over bowled by which Englishman?

3) England hosted the 2009 edition of the tournament and crashed to a shock defeat to which country in the opening match?

4) Despite that loss England qualified for the Super 8's stage in which they won a thriller by three runs against which side?

5) England went on to win the 2010 World Cup, but only qualified from their group on net run rate at the expense of which team?

6) England sealed their place in the final by beating which team in the Semis?

7) Who top scored for England in the 2010 Final against Australia with 63 runs?

8) Which England player was named as player of the tournament in 2010?

9) In their first match of the 2012 tournament England thrashed Afghanistan with which English batter making 99*?

10) England exited that World Cup when they lost their final Super Eight match against Sri Lanka with which opposition bowler taking five wickets?

11) England won only one match in the 2014 T20 World Cup, beating Sri Lanka thanks in part to which player scoring the first ever hundred for England in the T20 format?

12) Although they went on to reach the final in 2016, England lost their opening match to the West Indies when which opposition player scored a hundred?

13) England played out a thriller against South Africa in the 2016 Group Stage when they chased down what mammoth total to win the game?

14) Which side did England knock out at the Semi Final stage of that tournament?

15) In the 2016 Final which England bowler took two wickets in the second over of the West Indies reply?

16) Which West Indies batter top scored in their innings to help them reach their target and seal a dramatic victory?

17) Who famously hit four sixes in the final over of the match off Ben Stokes to claim the title for the West Indies?

18) England claimed some revenge by hammering the West Indies in their opening match of the 2021 tournament, bowling them out for 55 with which bowler taking four wickets for only two runs?

19) Jos Buttler scored 101* from only 67 balls in the Group Stage against which country?

20) England lost in the Semi Final in 2021, being knocked out by which team?

Champions Trophy

1) England were beaten in the Quarter Final of the 2000 Champions Trophy by which team?

2) In 2002 England exited at the Group Stage after finishing second in their group which contained which other two countries?

3) England secured their passage from the Group Stage in 2004 by beating Sri Lanka, which player scored a hundred for England that day?

4) Which team did England beat in the Semi Final of the 2004 tournament?

5) Which future international umpire played for England in the 2004 Final versus the West Indies?

6) The West Indies claimed a dramatic victory when which two lower order batsmen guided them home in the run chase?

7) Who was England's wicketkeeper during the 2006 Champions Trophy?

8) In which country was the 2009 Champions Trophy held?

9) In the 2013 tournament held in England, the hosts sealed qualification for the Semi's by beating New Zealand, but which batter scored 64 of 47 balls in the rain affected match?

10) Which team did England comfortably beat in their Semi Final in 2013?

11) In a Final reduced to 20 overs a side, which English bowler took 3 wickets for 20 runs?

12) India claimed the 2013 title by defending a total of 129, with an England collapse requiring which tail-ender to hit a six off the last ball, which he failed to do?

13) Which team did England beat in the opening match of the 2017 tournament, with Joe Root anchoring the chase with an unbeaten hundred?

14) Having already qualified for the Semi's, England then knocked Australia out by beating them in last Group Stage game, with which bowler taking 4/33?

15) England saw their hopes of winning their home tournament disappear when they were well beaten in the Semi Final by which team, who went onto win the Final themselves?

Debuts

1) Joe Root made his Test debut against which team in December 2012?

2) Against which country did Steve Harmison win his first Test cap in 2002?

3) Which wicketkeeper made a duck on his Test debut against New Zealand in June 2021?

4) Which player made his ODI debut versus Pakistan in 2001, going on to make a total of 197 appearances in that format?

5) Dawid Malan made a fifty on his T20 international debut against which side in 2017?

6) Which Yorkshire all-rounder made his Test Match debut against Zimbabwe in 2003, the game which also saw Jimmy Anderson pick up his first cap?

7) Who became England's first ever concussion substitute when he debuted against New Zealand in June 2022 when Jack Leach was forced to withdraw from the match?

8) Pace bowler Matt Potts also debuted in that game, taking the wicket of which New Zealand batsman as his first Test victim?

9) Ben Foakes made a hundred on his Test debut against which team in 2018?

10) Which pace bowler began his illustrious England career in a T20 against Pakistan in 2006?

Final Appearances

1) In what unusual manner did Alastair Cook reach a century in his final test match knock?

2) Michael Atherton was dismissed by which Australian in his final Test innings in 2001?

3) Who played his final Test against South Africa in 2008, registering a golden duck in the first innings?

4) Kevin Pietersen was never selected for England again after a Test series defeat against which country?

5) Which opposition player did Andrew Flintoff memorably run-out during his final ever Test?

6) Which batsman made his 100th and final test appearance against Bangladesh in 2005?

7) Alec Stewart finished his illustrious Test career with a victory over which team in 2003?

8) Which bowler made his final international appearance during the Fourth Test of the 2005 Ashes?

9) Ian Bell played his final games for England during a Test tour against which country?

10) Nasser Hussain scored a hundred in his final ever test innings against New Zealand in 2004, but which debutant opener was he involved in a run out with during that innings?

Test Cricket Part Two

1) How many deliveries did it take Johnny Bairstow to reach his sensational hundred against New Zealand at Trent Bridge in 2022 as the hosts chased down 299 for victory?

2) In an incredible coincidence, Stuart Broad and James Anderson dismissed the same West Indian batter to claim their 500th Test Match wickets, who was it?

3) England won their first ever day/night Test against which team at Edgbaston in 2017?

4) England amassed what massive score on their way to an innings victory over India at Edgbaston in 2011?

5) Which South African opener did James Anderson dismiss with the first ball of the Test series in December 2019?

6) Who took charge as interim Test head coach during the tour of the West Indies in 2022?

7) Which Indian batsman was run out for 99 by Alastair Cook during the 4th Test at Nagpur in December 2012?

8) Which Irish bowler claimed an historic 5/13 on the first day of the first ever Test between Ireland and England, at Lord's in 2019?

9) What scored did Zak Crawley eventually finish on in scoring a double century against Pakistan in August 2020?

10) Which spinner retired aged just 25 in 2017 to pursue other interests, having made his only three Test appearances the previous year?

11) Who top scored with 33 as England were skittled out for 58 in the first innings of the first Test away to New Zealand in March 2018?

12) Which IPL team was Brendon McCullum coaching when he was appointed England Test Coach in 2022?

13) Which Indian opener claimed a King pair at Edgbaston in 2011?

14) Which England bowler bowled what was reported to be the one millionth ever delivered in Test cricket?

15) Alastair Cook became England's all-time leading run scorer when he passed Graham Gooch's total of 8900 in a match versus which team in 2015?

16) Which part-time spinner claimed figures of five wickets for eight runs in the first innings of the 3rd Test away to India in 2021?

17) After surviving for 20 overs alongside Moeen Ali, Jimmy Anderson was dismissed with one ball of the Test match remaining to hand which country victory at Headingley in 2014?

18) Matt Prior and Monty Panesar held on to claim a draw against New Zealand at Auckland in 2013, but what was the final score of the three match series?

19) Which South African scored 311 against England at The Oval in July 2012?

20) Who dismissed Virat Kohli for a golden duck in the 1st Test against India at Trent Bridge in 2021?

One Day Internationals Part Two

1) Which three batters scored hundreds as England broke their own world record ODI score by hitting 498/4 against the Netherlands in June 2022?

2) Which wicketkeeper-batsman scored his first international hundred in an ODI against Australia in September 2020?

3) Which player hit a six off the last ball of the game as England claimed a dramatic tie against Sri Lanka in June 2016?

4) Which opener scored 180 off 151 balls against Australia in Melbourne in January 2018?

5) Jos Buttler reached a hundred off 46 balls against which country in 2015?

6) England lost by six runs to which non test playing nation in June 2018?

7) Which company was the main sponsor on England's ODI shirt during the 2015 World Cup?

8) Which fast bowler conceded just four runs off the last over as England beat South Africa by two runs at the Ageas Bowl in May 2017?

9) For what unusual reason was Ben Stokes given out during the ODI at Lord's versus Australia in 2015?

10) In their first game after the disastrous 2015 World Cup campaign, England started off an new era of aggressive batting in the series against New Zealand, but which opener was dismissed from the first ball of the match?

11) England clinched that series 3-2 when which batter came into the side in the final game and scored 83* off 60 balls to guide them home in the run chase?

12) England bowled Sri Lanka out for 67 at Old Trafford in May 2014, which bowler took five wickets that day?

13) Which all-rounder scored 102 off 57 balls versus the West Indies in September 2017?

14) England drew 2-2 in the away series against the West Indies in 2019, with which Windies batsman scoring two hundreds and another half century off just 19 balls?

15) By what series score did England beat Australia over five games during the opposition's one-day tour of England in 2018?

One Cap Wonders

Name the player who only won one England cap for either a test match or limited overs appearance from the description below

Test Caps:

1) Nottinghamshire seamer who played his only test against South Africa in 2008

2) Pace bowler who appeared for Ireland both before and after winning his sole England cap

3) Durham all-rounder picked to replace Graeme Swann in the 2013/14 Ashes

4) Slow left arm bowler who debuted alongside Chris Woakes in the final test of the 2013 Ashes

5) Seam bowler who earned 14 ODI caps alongside his only test appearance versus South Africa in 2003

6) Bowler who debuted against Sri Lanka in 2006, later going on to become bowling coach

7) Left-arm spinner who appeared in a test away to India in 2006, also earning 34 ODI caps

ODI Caps:

8) Off break bowler who made his solitary appearance in an ODI versus Sri Lanka in 2006

9) Long serving Lancashire bowler who earned his only England cap against Ireland in 2006

10) Nottinghamshire all-rounder who played one match against the West Indies in 2000

11) Slow left arm bowler who earned one ODI cap in 2012, although he also appeared seven times in T20 internationals

12) Consistent pace bowler who debuted against South Africa in 2017, making his only four test appearances later that year

T20 Caps:

13) Off spinner who's only T20 appearance came against South Africa in 2007, bowling just one over

14) Popular spinner who earned just one T20 cap, despite making 76 international appearances across tests and ODI's

15) Wicketkeeper who earned his only T20 cap aged 36 in 2007 who also played 19 ODI's in the same year

First Hundreds

Can you name the team that these players scored their first hundred for England against from the options below? Remember, this includes Test Matches, ODI's and T20's.

1) Marcus Trescothick
   Pakistan
   New Zealand
   Sri Lanka

2) Rob Key
   West Indies
   India
   South Africa

3) Kevin Pietersen
   Australia
   Bangladesh
   South Africa

4) Alastair Cook
   India
   Pakistan
   Bangladesh

5) Stuart Broad
   Australia
   India
   Pakistan

6) Joe Root
   Australia
   New Zealand
   India

7) Jonny Bairstow
   India
   South Africa
   Australia

8) Chris Woakes
   India
   Pakistan
   Sri Lanka

9) James Vince
   Pakistan
   Australia
   Bangladesh

10) Liam Livingstone
   India
   South Africa
   Pakistan

The Ashes Part Two

1) Who bowled a wide with the first delivery of the 2013 Ashes in England?

2) Number 11 Ashton Agar came within 2 runs of scoring an incredible hundred in the opening match of the 2013 series before being dismissed by which bowler?

3) Who took the most wickets during the 2013 series in England, with 26?

4) England retained the Ashes with a draw at which English ground in 2013?

5) Who took six wickets in the first innings of the 1st Test in the 2013/14 Ashes tour?

6) How many wickets did Mitchell Johnson take during the 2013/14 Ashes in Australia?

7) England fell 150 runs short in the 3rd Test in December 2013 despite a second innings ton from which batter?

8) Which England bowler retired after the 3rd Test in December 2013?

9) Alastair Cook fell four runs short of an Ashes hundred at home when he was bowled by which Australian in the first innings of the 2nd Test at Lords in 2015?

10) How many runs did Stuart Broad conceded in his incredible spell when he took eight wickets in the first innings of the 4th Test in the 2015 series?

11) What was the final Australian total in that innings?

12) Who won the player of the series award in 2015?

13) James Vince was run out by who when well set on 83 during the 1st Test at Brisbane in 2017?

14) England fell to an innings defeat in the 3rd Test in 2017 despite which two players scoring hundreds in the first innings?

15) Alastair Cook scored another away double hundred at which ground in 2017?

16) England lost the 1st Test in 2019 despite which of their players scoring a ton in the first innings?

17) How many hundreds did Steve Smith make during the 2019 Ashes?

18) In the famous Headingley Test of 2019 England were skittled out for what score in their first innings?

19) Which umpire turned down Nathan Lyon's LBW appeal against Ben Stokes as the match reached its thrilling conclusion?

20) What score did Jack Leach finish on in that incredible second innings?

21) Who was the top scorer during the 2021/22 Ashes despite not playing in every Test?

22) Which England bowler took 6/37 in the final Australian innings of the 2021/22 series?

23) Which of the five Tests in the 2021/22 series did England not lose?

24) Who made the only hundred for England during the 2021/22 Ashes?

25) Who was the last man out during the 2021/22 Ashes series as England went down to a 4-0 defeat?

Answers

Test Cricket Part One – Answers

1) England lost their first Test Match of the 21st century by an innings and 37 runs away from home against which team in January 2000?
South Africa

2) Which bowler took four wickets in one over versus the West Indies in August 2000?
Andy Caddick

3) Pakistan forfeited the fourth Test in August 2006 after being accused of ball tampering at which English ground?
The Oval

4) Which player took 7/12 in the First Test against the West Indies in Kingston in 2004 as England claimed a ten wicket victory?
Steve Harmison

5) Alec Stewart scored a hundred in his 100th Test against which country at Old Trafford in the year 2000?
West Indies

6) During the 2009/10 tour of South Africa, which number 11 batsman twice had to survive in the final over of the game to save matches for England?
Graham Onions

7) In which year did Brian Lara score his world record 400 runs against England?
2004

8) Which South African scored consecutive double hundreds in the 1st and 2nd Tests of their 2003 tour of England?
Graeme Smith

9) Wicket-keeper Geraint Jones was born in which country?
Papua New Guinea

10) Muttiah Muralitharan became the leading wicket-taker of all time in Test cricket when he passed Shane Warne by claiming which England batter as his 709th victim in December 2007?
Paul Collingwood

11) Which legendary West Indian fast bowler played his final Test against England at the Oval in August 2000?
Curtly Ambrose

12) Which Pakistani batsman was comically out hit-wicket by falling onto his stumps after attempting a sweep off Monty Panesar at Headingley in 2006?
Inzamam-ul-Haq

13) Led by captain Andrew Flintoff, England won the 3rd Test away in India in 2006 to claim a memorable 1-1 draw in the series, but which veteran off-spinner took the final wicket of the series?
Shaun Udal

14) England collapsed to an innings and 23 run defeat when they were bowled out for 51 in their second innings against which team in February 2009?
West Indies

15) Which England bowler ended the victory over South Africa in the 4th Test at Johannesburg in 2005 with a match-winning contribution of 12 wickets?
Matthew Hoggard

16) Who took charge of his first Test Match as England coach against the West Indies in 2007?
Peter Moores

17) Which England bowler took a wicket with the first ball of the Test when he dismissed Daren Ganga of the West Indies at Chester-le-Street in June 2007?
Ryan Sidebottom

18) Which legendary South African batsman did James Anderson dismiss to claim his 100th Test wicket in 2008?
Jacques Kallis

19) England claimed a memorable series victory away against Pakistan in 2000, with which two batsmen finishing not out as they chased down the total in near darkness in the 3rd and final Test?
Graham Thorpe and Nasser Hussain

20) Michael Vaughan lost his wicket by what unusual mode of dismissal during the 1st innings of the 3rd Test against India in Bangalore in 2001?
Handled the ball

One Day Internationals Part One – Answers

1) Who hit five sixes off the final five balls of the innings off the bowling of Yuvraj Singh in an ODI against India in 2007?
Dimitri Mascarenhas

2) Against which country did England sneak home by one wicket thanks to a small partnership between Darren Gough and Alan Mullally in February 2000?
Zimbabwe

3) England tied the final of the NatWest Series at Lord's against which team in 2005?
Australia

4) Which off spinner took a stunning catch to dismiss Shane Watson in the second final of the 2007 Commonwealth Bank series in Australia?
Jamie Dalrymple

5) Which bowler agonisingly missed out on a hat-trick on his ODI debut against Bangladesh in 2005 when his hat-trick delivery bounced on top of the stumps but did not remove either bail?
Chris Tremlett

6) New Zealand claimed a last ball victory in a controversial match in 2008 which was played in a tense atmosphere after which New Zealand batsman was controversially run out after colliding with Ryan Sidebottom?
Grant Elliott

7) England tied with South Africa at Bloemfontein in February 2005 after which bowler restricted the hosts to seven off the final over, despite seeing a no-ball hit for four off his first delivery?
Kabir Ali

8) Which seamer took a remarkable 5 for 15 off ten overs against Zimbabwe in January 2000?
Mark Ealham

9) England lost a day/night match away from home against which country by one run in January 2000?
South Africa

10) Nasser Hussain scored his highest one-day score of 115 in a thrilling match against which country in the 2002 NatWest Series final?
India

11) England conceded a match versus which team at Headingley in June 2001 after a pitch invasion towards the end of the game?
Pakistan

12) James Kirtley took a sensational diving catch with his left hand in a 2002 ODI versus which side?
India

13) England lost a one-day international against the West Indies at Lord's in July 2004 despite which two players scoring hundreds for them that day?
Andrew Strauss and Andrew Flintoff

14) Which all-rounder claimed figures of 6 for 31 off his ten overs in a match versus against Bangladesh in 2005?
Paul Collingwood

15) Against which country did Kevin Pietersen make his England ODI debut in 2004?
Zimbabwe

Twenty 20's – Answers

1) Which England bowler took four wickets in the T20 victory in England's first ever match in the format, beating Australia before the Ashes series in 2005?
Jon Lewis

2) Who scored 103 off 51 balls against New Zealand in November 2019?
Dawid Malan

3) Which bowler successfully defended 17 runs in the super over after England and New Zealand had tied another match, this time a T20 in 2019?
Chris Jordan

4) England beat the West Indies by 1 run in the 2nd match of their 2022 tour despite which bowler conceding 28 runs off the last over of the match?
Saqib Mahmood

5) England were skittled out for just 80 when chasing 171 for victory against which team in 2012?
India

6) England fought back to beat Australia by two runs in the 1st T20 in September 2020, thanks in part to who bowling the last over of the match and securing the win?
Tom Curran

7) Chris Woakes conceded only 7 runs in the final over as England beat which side by 3 runs away from home in November 2015?
Pakistan

8) Which bowler claimed four wickets and only conceded six runs against the West Indies in 2019?
Chris Jordan

9) In the next match of that series another England player took four wickets, this time for seven runs, but who was it?
David Willey

10) Despite only chasing 114, England lost by 25 runs to which country in September 2011?
West Indies

11) Which veteran Sri Lankan opener claimed the man of the match award as England lost for the first time in T20 internationals in June 2006?
Sanath Jayasuriya

12) Which country did England beat 3-0 in an away series in late 2020?
South Africa

13) Which Australian opener smashed 156 off 63 balls in a T20 in 2013 as his team racked up a massive 248/6?
Aaron Finch

14) South Africa snuck home by running two off the last ball in the 1st match of the 2016 series after which England bowler failed to collect a throw from the deep to effect a run-out?
Reece Topley

15) Before becoming head coach of England's white ball team in 2022, Matthew Mott was the coach of which women's national side?
Australia

The Ashes Part One – Answers

1) At which ground did Mark Butcher score an unbeaten 173 to guide England to victory in the 4th Test in 2001?
Headingley

2) Who was the top wicket-taker during the 2001 Ashes?
Glenn McGrath

3) Which Australian made 152 in the 1st Test in 2001?
Adam Gilchrist

4) Which future Sky Sports Cricket presenter was dropped after the 3rd Test of the 2001 series and never played for England again?
Ian Ward

5) Which England bowler was injured in the outfield during the 1st Test of the 2002/03 series?
Simon Jones

6) Which Englishman was top scorer in the 2002/03 series in Australia with 633 runs?
Michael Vaughan

7) Who stood in for Alex Stewart as the England wicketkeeper for the 4th Test of the 2002/03 Ashes?
James Foster

8) Which bowler took seven second innings wickets to lead England to victory in the final Test in 2003?
Andy Caddick

9) Which four England players scored hundreds during the 2005 Ashes?
Andrew Strauss, Michael Vaughan, Kevin Pietersen and Andrew Flintoff

10) Which substitute fielder famously ran-out Ricky Ponting during the 4th Test in 2005?
Gary Pratt

11) How many wickets did Shane Warne take in the 2005 series?
40

12) At which ground did England win to take a 2-1 lead in the 2005 series?
Trent Bridge

13) Who scored a double hundred for England at Adelaide in the 2nd Test in 2006?
Paul Collingwood

14) Which two Australians combined to put on a partnership of 279 for the 6th wicket in the 2006 Boxing Day Test?
Matthew Hayden and Andrew Symonds

15) Which Australian pace bowler took 26 wickets in the 2006/07 series, more than anybody else?
Stuart Clark

16) England clung on for a draw in the 1st Test in 2009 after seeing which four Australians rack up tons in their only innings of the match?
Simon Katich, Ricky Ponting, Marcus North and Brad Haddin

17) Which batter helped keep Australia at bay in that 2009 Test by facing 245 balls in the second innings?
Paul Collingwood

18) With the first two deliveries of day two of the 3rd Test in 2009, which England bowler dismissed Shane Watson and Michael Hussey?
Graham Onions

19) England re-claimed the Ashes in 2009, with which player taking the final catch as Graeme Swann dismissed Michael Hussey?
Alastair Cook

20) What was the final series score in 2009?
England 2-1 Australia

21) Which three players did Peter Siddle dismiss for his hat-trick during the 1st Test of the 2010/11 series?
Alastair Cook, Matt Prior and Stuart Broad

22) Simon Katich was run-out in the first over of the 2nd Test in 2010 without facing a ball by which England fielder?
Jonathan Trott

23) At what score did England declare their second innings in the 1st Test of the 2010/11 Ashes?
517/1

24) How many runs did Alastair Cook score in the 2010/11 series?
766

25) Which England bowler took the final wicket of the series in 2010/11, dismissing Michael Beer to claim a 3-1 win?
Chris Tremlett

Captains – Answers

1) Who was the permanent England Test Match captain at the start of the 21st century?
Nasser Hussain

2) Graham Thorpe captained England in three One Day Internationals in 2001 against which team?
Sri Lanka

3) Who stood in as Test captain to replace Michael Vaughan on two occasions, once against New Zealand in 2004 and again versus Pakistan in 2005?
Marcus Trescothick

4) In which year did Andrew Strauss first captain the Test side?
2006 (As a stand-in for Andrew Flintoff)

5) Kevin Pietersen recorded how many wins as captain of the England Test team?
One

6) Which off spinner captained England in one T20 match against New Zealand in 2013, although the game was called off after two deliveries?
James Tredwell

7) Who was the permanent captain of the T20 side from 2011-2014?
Stuart Broad

8) Against which team did Joe Root begin his spell as England Test captain?
South Africa

9) Ben Stokes led England in a Test Match against which country in place of Joe Root in the summer of 2020?
West Indies

10) Ben Stokes returned to lead the ODI team in a three match series against Pakistan in 2021 after the initial squad was hit by a Covid-19 outbreak, but what was the final score of that series? **England 3-0 Pakistan**

First Wickets – Answers

1) Matthew Hoggard
   Younis Khan

2) Simon Jones
   Ajay Ratra

3) James Anderson
   Adam Gilchrist

4) Graeme Swann
   Kumar Sangakkara

5) Alistair Cook
   Ishant Sharma

6) Ben Stokes
   Shaun Marsh

7) Mark Wood
   William Porterfield

8) Craig Overton
   Steve Smith

9) Jofra Archer
Mark Adair

10) Matthew Fisher
John Campbell

50 Over World Cups – Answers

1) Andrew Flintoff was suspended by England during which years' World Cup after a drunken incident with a pedalo?
2007

2) Shoaib Akhtar bowled a delivery recorded at over 100mph to which England player during the group stage of the 2003 World Cup?
Nick Knight

3) Which Essex player took three wickets in the win over Namibia in 2003?
Ronnie Irani

4) Which Australian took seven wickets in the final Group Stage match as England were eliminated from the 2003 competition?
Andy Bichel

5) Which three teams did England face in the Group Stage of the 2007 World Cup?
New Zealand, Canada and Kenya

6) Which former and future Ireland international opened the batting for England at the 2007 World Cup?
Ed Joyce

7) Which England player scored tons versus Australia and West Indies in 2007?
Kevin Pietersen

8) In the 2011 competition England tied a Group Stage match against which team?
India

9) Which Irish player scored a dramatic hundred as England fell to an historic defeat in 2011?
Kevin O'Brien

10) Which two Sri Lankans scored unbeaten tons as England were beaten by 10 wickets at the Quarter Final stage in 2011?
Upul Tharanga and Tillakaratne Dilshan

11) England won only two of their six matches at the 2015 World Cup as they crashed out at the Group Stage, which teams did they beat?
Scotland and Afghanistan

12) Which batsman was left stranded on 98 not out during England's opening loss to Australia in 2015?
James Taylor

13) Which New Zealand batter scored 77 off 25 balls as they destroyed England in their 2015 meeting?
Brendon McCullum

14) Who was the last man to be dismissed as Bangladesh knocked England out of the 2015 competition by beating them by 15 runs?
James Anderson

15) Ben Stokes took an incredible catch to dismiss which South African in the opening day win in the 2019 World Cup?
Andile Phehlukwayo

16) England lost to Pakistan in the 2019 Group Stage despite which two of their batters scoring hundreds?
Joe Root and Jos Buttler

17) After England were hit by numerous injuries, who ended up batting at three in the win over the West Indies in 2019?
Chris Woakes

18) Which side did England beat in their final Group Stage game in 2019 to seal their Semi-Final place?
New Zealand

19) What score did both teams make in their 50 overs as England tied with New Zealand in the 2019 final?
241

20) Which England player fielded the ball in the deep then threw the ball to Jos Buttler off the last ball of the super over to claim victory for England in the 2019 World Cup Final?
Jason Roy

T20 World Cups – Answers

1) The first ever T20 World Cup was held in 2007, but which country was the host?
South Africa

2) In the match with India, Yuvraj Singh hit six sixes off one over bowled by which Englishman?
Stuart Broad

3) England hosted the 2009 edition of the tournament and crashed to a shock defeat to which country in the opening match?
Netherlands

4) Despite that loss England qualified for the Super 8's stage in which they won a thriller by three runs against which side?
India

5) England went on to win the 2010 World Cup, but only qualified from their group on net run rate at the expense of which team?
Ireland

6) England sealed their place in the final by beating which team in the Semis?
Sri Lanka

7) Who top scored for England in the 2010 Final against Australia with 63 runs?
Craig Kieswetter

8) Which England player was named as player of the tournament in 2010?
Kevin Pietersen

9) In their first match of the 2012 tournament England thrashed Afghanistan with which English batter making 99*?
Luke Wright

10) England exited that World Cup when they lost their final Super Eight match against Sri Lanka with which opposition bowler taking five wickets?
Lasith Malinga

11) England won only one match in the 2014 T20 World Cup, beating Sri Lanka thanks in part to which player scoring the first ever hundred for England in the T20 format?
Alex Hales

12) Although they went on to reach the final in 2016, England lost their opening match to the West Indies when which opposition player scored a hundred?
Chris Gayle

13) England played out a thriller against South Africa in the 2016 Group Stage when they chased down what mammoth total to win the game?
229

14) Which side did England knock out at the Semi Final stage of that tournament?
New Zealand

15) In the 2016 Final which England bowler took two wickets in the second over of the West Indies reply?
Joe Root

16) Which West Indies batter top scored in their innings to help them reach their target and seal a dramatic victory?
Marlon Samuels

17) Who famously hit four sixes in the final over of the match off Ben Stokes to claim the title for the West Indies?
Carlos Brathwaite

18) England claimed some revenge by hammering the West Indies in their opening match of the 2021 tournament, bowling them out for 55 with which bowler taking four wickets for only two runs?

Adil Rashid

19) Jos Buttler scored 101* from only 67 balls in the Group Stage against which country?

Sri Lanka

20) England lost in the Semi Final in 2021, being knocked out by which team?

New Zealand

Champions Trophy – Answers

1) England were beaten in the Quarter Final of the 2000 Champions Trophy by which team?
South Africa

2) In 2002 England exited at the Group Stage after finishing second in their group which contained which other two countries?
India and Zimbabwe

3) England secured their passage from the Group Stage in 2004 by beating Sri Lanka, which player scored a hundred for England that day?
Andrew Flintoff

4) Which team did England beat in the Semi Final of the 2004 tournament?
Australia

5) Which future international umpire played for England in the 2004 Final versus the West Indies?
Alex Wharf

6) The West Indies claimed a dramatic victory when which two lower order batsmen guided them home in the run chase?
Courtney Browne and Ian Bradshaw

7) Who was England's wicketkeeper during the 2006 Champions Trophy?
Chris Read

8) In which country was the 2009 Champions Trophy held?
South Africa

9) In the 2013 tournament held in England, the hosts sealed qualification for the Semi's by beating New Zealand, but which batter scored 64 of 47 balls in the rain affected match?
Alastair Cook

10) Which team did England comfortably beat in their Semi Final in 2013?
South Africa

11) In a Final reduced to 20 overs a side, which English bowler took 3 wickets for 20 runs?
Ravi Bopara

12) India claimed the 2013 title by defending a total of 129, with an England collapse requiring which tail-ender to hit a six off the last ball, which he failed to do?
James Tredwell

13) Which team did England beat in the opening match of the 2017 tournament, with Joe Root anchoring the chase with an unbeaten hundred?
Bangladesh

14) Having already qualified for the Semi's, England then knocked Australia out by beating them in last Group Stage game, with which bowler taking 4/33?
Mark Wood

15) England saw their hopes of winning their home tournament disappear when they were well beaten in the Semi Final by which team, who went onto win the Final themselves?
Pakistan

Debuts – Answers

1) Joe Root made his Test debut against which team in December 2012?
   India

2) Against which country did Steve Harmison win his first Test cap in 2002?
   India

3) Which wicketkeeper made a duck on his Test debut against New Zealand in June 2021?
   James Bracey

4) Which player made his ODI debut versus Pakistan in 2001, going on to make a total of 197 appearances in that format?
   Paul Collingwood

5) Dawid Malan made a fifty on his T20 international debut against which side in 2017?
   South Africa

6) Which Yorkshire all-rounder made his Test Match debut against Zimbabwe in 2003, the game which also saw Jimmy Anderson pick up his first cap?
Anthony McGrath

7) Who became England's first ever concussion substitute when he debuted against New Zealand in June 2022 when Jack Leach was forced to withdraw from the match?
Matt Parkinson

8) Pace bowler Matt Potts also debuted in that game, taking the wicket of which New Zealand batsman as his first Test victim?
Kane Williamson

9) Ben Foakes made a hundred on his Test debut against which team in 2018?
Sri Lanka

10) Which pace bowler began his illustrious England career in a T20 against Pakistan in 2006?
Stuart Broad

Final Appearances – Answers

1) In what unusual manner did Alastair Cook reach a century in his final test match knock?
With overthrows

2) Michael Atherton was dismissed by which Australian in his final Test innings in 2001?
Glenn McGrath

3) Who played his final Test against South Africa in 2008, registering a golden duck in the first innings?
Michael Vaughan

4) Kevin Pietersen was never selected for England again after a Test series defeat against which country?
Australia

5) Which opposition player did Andrew Flintoff memorably run-out during his final ever Test?
Ricky Ponting

6) Which batsman made his 100th and final test appearance against Bangladesh in 2005?
Graham Thorpe

7) Alec Stewart finished his illustrious Test career with a victory over which team in 2003?
South Africa

8) Which bowler made his final international appearance during the Fourth Test of the 2005 Ashes?
Simon Jones

9) Ian Bell played his final games for England during a Test tour against which country?
Pakistan

10) Nasser Hussain scored a hundred in his final ever test innings against New Zealand in 2004, but which debutant opener was he involved in a run out with during that innings?

Andrew Strauss

Test Cricket Part Two – Answers

1) How many deliveries did it take Johnny Bairstow to reach his sensational hundred against New Zealand at Trent Bridge in 2022 as the hosts chased down 299 for victory?
   77

2) In an incredible coincidence, Stuart Broad and James Anderson dismissed the same West Indian batter to claim their 500th Test Match wickets, who was it?
   Kraigg Brathwaite

3) England won their first ever day/night Test against which team at Edgbaston in 2017?
   West Indies

4) England amassed what massive score on their way to an innings victory over India at Edgbaston in 2011?
   710/7 declared

5) Which South African opener did James Anderson dismiss with the first ball of the Test series in December 2019?
Dean Elgar

6) Who took charge as interim Test head coach during the tour of the West Indies in 2022?
Paul Collingwood

7) Which Indian batsman was run out for 99 by Alastair Cook during the 4th Test at Nagpur in December 2012?
MS Dhoni

8) Which Irish bowler claimed an historic 5/13 on the first day of the first ever Test between Ireland and England, at Lord's in 2019?
Tim Murtagh

9) What scored did Zak Crawley eventually finish on in scoring a double century against Pakistan in August 2020?
267

10) Which spinner retired aged just 25 in 2017 to pursue other interests, having made his only three Test appearances the previous year?
Zafar Ansari

11) Who top scored with 33 as England were skittled out for 58 in the first innings of the first Test away to New Zealand in March 2018?
Craig Overton

12) Which IPL team was Brendon McCullum coaching when he was appointed England Test Coach in 2022?
Kolkata Knight Riders

13) Which Indian opener claimed a King pair at Edgbaston in 2011?
Virender Sehwag

14) Which England bowler bowled what was reported to be the one millionth ever delivered in Test cricket?
Ben Stokes (David Warner hit it for four)

15) Alastair Cook became England's all-time leading run scorer when he passed Graham Gooch's total of 8900 in a match versus which team in 2015?
New Zealand

16) Which part-time spinner claimed figures of five wickets for eight runs in the first innings of the 3rd Test away to India in 2021?
Joe Root

17) After surviving for 20 overs alongside Moeen Ali, Jimmy Anderson was dismissed with one ball of the Test match remaining to hand which country victory at Headingley in 2014?
Sri Lanka

18) Matt Prior and Monty Panesar held on to claim a draw against New Zealand at Auckland in 2013, but what was the final score of the three match series?
New Zealand 0-0 England

19) Which South African scored 311 against England at The Oval in July 2012?
Hashim Amla

20) Who dismissed Virat Kohli for a golden duck in the 1st Test against India at Trent Bridge in 2021?
Jimmy Anderson

**One Day Internationals Part Two –
Answers**

1) Which three batters scored hundreds as
    England broke their own world record
    ODI score by hitting 498/4 against the
    Netherlands in June 2022?
    Phil Salt, Dawid Malan and Jos Buttler

2) Which wicketkeeper-batsman scored his
    first international hundred in an ODI
    against Australia in September 2020?
    Sam Billings

3) Which player hit a six off the last ball of
    the game as England claimed a dramatic
    tie against Sri Lanka in June 2016?
    Liam Plunkett

4) Which opener scored 180 off 151 balls
    against Australia in Melbourne in
    January 2018?
    Jason Roy

5) Jos Buttler reached a hundred off 46 balls against which country in 2015?
Pakistan

6) England lost by six runs to which non test playing nation in June 2018?
Scotland

7) Which company was the main sponsor on England's ODI shirt during the 2015 World Cup?
Waitrose

8) Which fast bowler conceded just four runs off the last over as England beat South Africa by two runs at the Ageas Bowl in May 2017?
Mark Wood

9) For what unusual reason was Ben Stokes given out during the ODI at Lord's versus Australia in 2015?
Obstructing the field

10) In their first game after the disastrous 2015 World Cup campaign, England started off an new era of aggressive batting in the series against New Zealand, but which opener was dismissed from the first ball of the match?
Jason Roy

11) England clinched that series 3-2 when which batter came into the side in the final game and scored 83* off 60 balls to guide them home in the run chase?
Jonny Bairstow

12) England bowled Sri Lanka out for 67 at Old Trafford in May 2014, which bowler took five wickets that day?
Chris Jordan

13) Which all-rounder scored 102 off 57 balls versus the West Indies in September 2017?
Moeen Ali

14) England drew 2-2 in the away series against the West Indies in 2019, with which Windies batsman scoring two hundreds and another half century off just 19 balls?
Chris Gayle

15) By what series score did England beat Australia over five games during the opposition's one-day tour of England in 2018?
England 5-0 Australia

One Cap Wonders – Answers

Name the player who only won one England cap for either a test match or limited overs appearance from the description below

Test Caps:

1) Nottinghamshire seamer who played his only test against South Africa in 2008
   Darren Pattinson

2) Pace bowler who appeared for Ireland both before and after winning his sole England cap
   Boyd Rankin

3) Durham all-rounder picked to replace Graeme Swann in the 2013/14 Ashes
   Scott Borthwick

4) Slow left arm bowler who debuted alongside Chris Woakes in the final test of the 2013 Ashes
   Simon Kerrigan

5) Seam bowler who earned 14 ODI caps alongside his only test appearance versus South Africa in 2003
Kabir Ali

6) Bowler who debuted against Sri Lanka in 2006, later going on to become bowling coach
Jon Lewis

7) Left-arm spinner who appeared in a test away to India in 2006, also earning 34 ODI caps
Ian Blackwell

ODI Caps:

8) Off break bowler who made his solitary appearance in an ODI versus Sri Lanka in 2006
Alex Loudon

9) Long serving Lancashire bowler who earned his only England cap against Ireland in 2006
Glen Chapple

10) Nottinghamshire all-rounder who played one match against the West Indies in 2000
Paul Franks

11) Slow left arm bowler who earned one ODI cap in 2012, although he also appeared seven times in T20 internationals
Danny Briggs

12) Consistent pace bowler who debuted against South Africa in 2017, making his only four test appearances later that year
Toby Roland-Jones

T20 Caps:

13) Off spinner who's only T20 appearance
came against South Africa in 2007,
bowling just one over
Jeremy Snape

14) Popular spinner who earned just one
T20 cap, despite making 76 international
appearances across tests and ODI's
Monty Panesar

15) Wicketkeeper who earned his only T20
cap aged 36 in 2007 who also played 19
ODI's in the same year
Paul Nixon

First Hundreds – Answers

1) Marcus Trescothick
   Sri Lanka

2) Rob Key
   West Indies

3) Kevin Pietersen
   South Africa

4) Alastair Cook
   India

5) Stuart Broad
   Pakistan

6) Joe Root
   New Zealand

7) Jonny Bairstow
   South Africa

8) Chris Woakes
   India

9) James Vince
   Pakistan

10) Liam Livingstone
    Pakistan

The Ashes Part Two – Answers

1) Who bowled a wide with the first delivery of the 2013 Ashes in England?
James Pattinson

2) Number 11 Ashton Agar came within 2 runs of scoring an incredible hundred in the opening match of the 2013 series before being dismissed by which bowler?
Stuart Broad

3) Who took the most wickets during the 2013 series in England, with 26?
Graeme Swann

4) England retained the Ashes with a draw at which English ground in 2013?
Old Trafford

5) Who took six wickets in the first innings of the 1st Test in the 2013/14 Ashes tour?
Stuart Broad

6) How many wickets did Mitchell Johnson take during the 2013/14 Ashes in Australia?
37

7) England fell 150 runs short in the 3rd Test in December 2013 despite a second innings ton from which batter?
Ben Stokes

8) Which England bowler retired after the 3rd Test in December 2013?
Graeme Swann

9) Alastair Cook fell four runs short of an Ashes hundred at home when he was bowled by which Australian in the first innings of the 2nd Test at Lords in 2015?
Mitchell Marsh

10) How many runs did Stuart Broad conceded in his incredible spell when he took eight wickets in the first innings of the 4th Test in the 2015 series?
15

11) What was the final Australian total in that innings?
60

12) Who won the player of the series award in 2015?
Joe Root

13) James Vince was run out by who when well set on 83 during the 1st Test at Brisbane in 2017?
Nathan Lyon

14) England fell to an innings defeat in the 3rd Test in 2017 despite which two players scoring hundreds in the first innings?
Dawid Malan and Jonny Bairstow

15) Alastair Cook scored another away double hundred at which ground in 2017?
The MCG

16) England lost the 1st Test in 2019 despite which of their players scoring a ton in the first innings?
Rory Burns

17) How many hundreds did Steve Smith make during the 2019 Ashes?
Three

18) In the famous Headingley Test of 2019 England were skittled out for what score in their first innings?
67

19) Which umpire turned down Nathan Lyon's LBW appeal against Ben Stokes as the match reached its thrilling conclusion?
Joel Wilson

20) What score did Jack Leach finish on in that incredible second innings?
One

21) Who was the top scorer during the 2021/22 Ashes despite not playing in every Test?
Travis Head

22) Which England bowler took 6/37 in the final Australian innings of the 2021/22 series?
Mark Wood

23) Which of the five Tests in the 2021/22 series did England not lose?
The Fourth Test

24) Who made the only hundred for England during the 2021/22 Ashes?
Jonny Bairstow

25) Who was the last man out during the 2021/22 Ashes series as England went down to a 4-0 defeat?
Ollie Robinson

If you enjoyed this book please consider leaving a five star review on Amazon

Made in the USA
Middletown, DE
20 December 2022

19595841R00068